Christ In You

To include:

Christ In Man
Christ Is Your Life
Christ Bears Our Sins
Christ Unveiled

Neville Goddard

Contents

Christ In You

"Examine yourselves to see if you are holding to your faith. Test yourselves! Do you not realize that Jesus Christ is in you?" Now, faith is not complete until through experiment it becomes experience! When you test the Christ in you and prove from experience that it works, then you have the faith. But first you must find who Christ is, where he is, and what he is. You are not called upon to test a tradition of man as something on the outside, but Jesus Christ who is in you!

Perhaps you heard on the news tonight that the Catholics have just eliminated forty saints. For hundreds of years millions of people have prayed to Saint Christopher, yet now they are being told that he never existed. How many St. Christopher medals and figurines were sold to protect those who went into battle or traveled afar? Believing he was the saint of the traveler, how many put their faith in him? Santa Barbara was named after Saint Barb, who is now believed to be non-existent, yet the cause of the recent broken oil line!

If you will read scripture carefully (and not go along with the herd) you will see that there is no intermediary between yourself and God. No priest or saint, minister, truth teacher, or so-called healer can be an intermediary between you and God. Christ in you is your hope of glory. You must examine yourself to see if you are holding to this faith. Test yourself. Do you not realize that Jesus Christ is in you? If you do, put him to the test. He is your power to create, your power to imagine everything - be it good, bad, or indifferent.

The 14th chapter of the Book of John begins: "Let not your hearts be troubled." This statement is repeated in different ways over and over again by the master of souls - who is Christ in you, for when he awakens fear is abolished. Awake, he urges you to fear not, be not afraid, be not troubled. A tyrant could not exist without fear. He must scare us to death before he can rule us. By slaughtering millions (and you are afraid you will be next) he has you under his power. But if you know you and your family cannot die, you will not be afraid and there would be no tyrant. Tyranny can exist only in a frightened world. So, Awakened Imagination begins the 14th (chapter) of John by saying: "Let not your heart be troubled, you believe in God, believe also in me. In my Father's house are many mansions. If it were not so would I have told you that I go to prepare a place for you? And when I go and prepare a place for you, I will come again and take you to myself, that where I am there you may be also. Now the place you know and the way you know." Then Thomas said, 'Lord, we do not know where you are going, so how can we know the way?' and he replied, 'I am the way and the truth and the life.' Then Philip said, 'Show us the Father and we will be satisfied.' And he answered, 'I have been so long with you and yet you do not know me Philip? He who has seen me has seen the Father. How then can you say, 'Show us the Father?'"

Let us take this verse on this level first and then take it into the higher level. In my Father's house are many mansions. The word translated "mansion" means to stay in a certain place; state; relation; or expectancy." There are infinite states from which you may view the world. You may enter a state and abide there until it becomes your home or you could be simply passing through for a moment, but it is a state, one of your Father's mansions. Choose the mansion in your Father's house that you would like to enter. Assume you are already there. Feel the reality of the state surround you and you have arrived. Your dream is now true, but you must abide there!

When you leave this auditorium tonight you expect to return to the place you left to come here. At the moment this auditorium is solid and real, while your home is only a mental image. So what is a home? It is the state to which your thoughts most constantly return. Are you thinking from the state you desire? Or is your dream just a passing fancy, a daydream you enjoyed for the moment and then dropped? You can tell if you abide in your house of desire by watching your thoughts, for the state in which you most constantly return constitutes your dwelling place.

When you imagined you were the person you wanted to be and heard your friends rejoice at your good fortune, you entered that state and prepared a place in which to dwell; for at that moment Christ in you was speaking to the outer, rational you. As your own wonderful human imagination Christ is telling you that he knows you are afraid, that you have obligations in life which must be met, but to not be afraid for "I will go and prepare a place for you." Knowing this, close your physical eyes upon the world round about you and let not your heart be troubled, neither let it be afraid, for all things are possible to Christ in you! Let him prepare the state, for he is the way to its fulfillment.

Closing your eyes against the facts of life, dare to assume you are seeing and hearing what you would see and hear if your desire were true. Now, tune it in as you would a radio. If, when you turned on the radio four or five stations are heard at the same time, you couldn't stand the confusion and would turn the radio off. So it is with your imagination - it must be fine-tuned. Now no radio or TV is comparable to you, for that which the mind creates cannot be greater than the mind who created it. We are amazed at the perfection of a little instrument called a radio because it can produce sound out of the nowhere, yet the mind that is so amazed is the one who created it. Our radio or television can be carried around the house or yard with no connection to a charge of electricity, yet the sound and picture come through perfect, and any station (or channel) can be reached by merely a flick of the wrist. At this moment everything that is being broadcast or telecast in the world is in this room, but we haven't tuned it in.

Now, you have an instrument infinitely greater than any radio or television, but it must be turned on and fine-tuned. Think of a friend who would truly rejoice in your good fortune. Tune him in until his is the only voice you can hear. Let him tell you of his thrill because of your good fortune. Listen carefully until his voice is crystal clear and you can hear the sentence you put upon that voice. Now, believe in its reality. If you will, you are living by this principle and not merely accepting the Christian faith as a substitute for living by it.

Can you imagine the turmoil which is going on in the Catholic world tonight now that the courts have cut off forty of their so-called saints? Half of my family is Catholic. I do hope that my Protestant brothers, who did not marry Catholic girls, will be big enough to mention it. I recall about twenty years ago my wife and I visited a Catholic family. At the time my wife said to me: "They are ardent Catholics, but don't know a thing about you except that you are a Protestant and not saved." After a lovely dinner we sat around the pool and watched their three sons swim. Each boy wore a St. Christopher's medal around his neck. One was three years into the priesthood when he quit, joined the army, and returned minus his hearing. Another returned without a foot and the third minus an arm. They told me that they believed that without this medal they would have died. Well, I wonder what will happen to that family when they learn St. Christopher never existed! The only Christ who ever existed is within you as your own wonderful human imagination. There never was another.

When one being awoke to discover all that was foretold in scripture was taking place in him, he knew who the Messiah really was. He told his story, while some believed and some did not believe him. Those who heard and believed him wrote his experiences in the form of a story, because truth is far more acceptable when told in story form, as in our four gospels. But one day we will be big enough to hear it without the story form to support us.

Redemption was foretold in the Old Testament, but not understood by those who recorded it. The prophets who prophesied the coming of the Messiah searched and inquired concerning this grace that was to be ours, and it was revealed to them that it was not for them to know. The time had not yet come, for it was for us. Now that the horrors have been fulfilled, the Messiah who was buried in us before that the world was is beginning to erupt in the individual. Everything said of Jesus Christ will be realized in you individually, for the Bible was written about you.

Now, before the Messiah comes, you can put his word to the test. If Christ is your own wonderful human imagination and all things - be they good, bad, or indifferent - are made by him, you can imagine unlovely things and perpetuate their image. To say that Christ makes only the good and a devil makes the evil is false, for the devil is just as phony as Christopher. When you doubt the power of Christ in you - that's the devil. Unless you actually believe that "I am" is the being you are seeking and pray only to him by exercising your human imagination, you will never reach your desire, for awareness is the only power that can give it to you.

Tonight, ask yourself what you would be aware of hearing, seeing and experiencing if your desire were now fulfilled. If what I tell you is true and your imagination is the creator of all things, then you should be able to prove his power in the testing. I tell you: there is no intermediary between yourself and God. If you will but test this power within you, it will prove itself in performance. Then you will know who Christ really is.

Now, no one comes unto the Father except by me and I am going to tell you exactly how to come to the Father. It is not spelled out in scripture. I searched, but could not find him until he revealed himself to me. One day he will reveal himself in you, for you will see a lad, chosen by God to be his son. The lad will be ruddy in complexion, very handsome, with beautiful eyes. He will be in his early teens. As you look into his eyes you know exactly who he is and who you are. Then and only then do you know you are God the Father. So, no one comes to the awareness of being God the Father except by the revelation of David, for he is the one through whom you come to the awareness of Fatherhood.

In this same 14th chapter of John, Awakened Imagination asks this question: "I have been so long with you and yet you do not know me? He who has seen me has seen the Father, how then can you say, 'Show us the Father?" David is one with his father. He is united to the Lord, having become one spirit with him. So, the only way you can ever find the Father within you is to bring forth his son, David. We are told in the 89th Psalm: "I have found David. He has cried unto me 'Thou art my Father, my God and the Rock of my salvation.'"

The word "found" recorded here, if taken on the surface implies David was lost; but the word means, "to bring forth one who is behind you." David, eternal youth, was put into the mind of man, yet so that man cannot find out what God has done from the beginning to the end when he brings forth that which was behind all along, waiting to come out. You will never know you are God the Father until David appears and calls you Father. It is he who stated in the 2nd Psalm: "I will tell of the decree of the Lord, he said unto me, 'Thou art my son, today I have begotten thee.'" In my own case I felt an explosion in my skull, and when everything settled, I saw my son leaning against the side of an open door, looking out on a pastoral scene. As he turned and looked at me standing at his right, I knew I was his father, fulfilling scripture.

The gospel is the truest story ever told but men, because of their traditions, have voided the world of God and built a stupid concept called "saints." What man on earth could be a saint? The only saints are the redeemed, those who form the body of the Risen Lord. May I tell you: everyone is predestined for that redemption. Not one will be lost, so why pick someone out and call him a saint only to later deny he was ever a Christian? They even took Saint Nicolas off their list, claiming he never existed! Here are mortal men, without vision, appointing themselves judges of saints!

I tell you: regardless of what you do here as a mortal man you are redeemed, for redemption hasn't a thing to do with the man's ethical code. It's entirely up to the being within a man who - having played all the parts - awakens to receive the crown of righteousness which has been waiting for your return. The moment he awakens you are redeemed. But your friends know you as mortal and have not the slightest concept of what this power is. Browning said in his "Reverie":

From the first, Power was - I knew
That, strive but for a closer view,
Love were as plain to see.

This is true for: prior to power, was love. In my own case striving for love did not reveal it to me. Only when God in me unveiled himself as love was it plain to see.

As love, you will exercise your almighty power in the world to come. To have that power here, before you were incorporated into the body of love, would cause havoc in the world; for the God of whom I speak is infinite love and almighty power, and that God you are, but you will not know it until your journey is complete. Only when he completes the journey will he unveil himself to you - his emanation - by embracing you into his own being. At that moment you will cease to be another, for you will become one with the Living God. Then you will tell your story to all who will listen. Some will believe you and others will disbelieve, but you will tell it until you take off your mortal garment for the last time to become one with the Risen Lord who is made up of all the redeemed of humanity. And in the end, when all are redeemed, this being who was before that the world was will be more powerful, more wise, and more glorious, because of his journey into the world of death.

Tonight, learn to fine-tune your imagination. Knowing the voice of your friend, tune him in. Determine the words you want him to say and listen carefully. Tune him in until his words are fine and clear, then believe you heard him. Think it really happened. If you will, it will come to pass. When, I cannot say, for every imaginal act is like an egg and no two eggs (unless they are of the same species) have the same interval of time for hatching. The little bird comes out in three weeks, a sheep in five months, a horse in twelve months, and a human in nine months. Your imaginal act has its own appointed hour to ripen and flower. If it seems long, wait - for it is sure and will not be late for itself.

An imaginal act is a creative act, for the moment it is felt, the seed (or state) is fertilized. It will take a certain length of time to be born, so start today by assuming you are the man (or woman) you would like to be and let the people in your mind's eye reflect the truth of your assumption. Be faithful to your assumption. Persist in this thought, for persistence is the way to bring your desire to pass. You don't persist through effort or fear, rather knowing that your imaginal act is now a fact; wait for its birth, for it will come.

Now, a friend wrote, saying that in her dream she was walking down the street holding a fish in her hands. The fish appeared to be dead, yet she could feel it pulse. Determine to keep the fish alive, she found a cup, filled it with water, and placed the fish inside. Then she awoke, hearing a male voice say: "Oh my darling."

Every dream contains within itself the capacity for symbolic significance. A fish is the symbol of the power of the human imagination. Imagine yourself depressed, and imagination will throw you into the pit of depression. Imagine yourself free, and your imaginative power will bring you out, for your imagination is the savior of your world. When you become lost in the reasoning world, your imagination is not fed with your desire, for reason negates its flow. Christ, being your human imagination, is not limited by the reasoning world and all things are possible to him. If you would ignore the facts and walk in your imaginal acts as though your wish were already fulfilled you are feeding Christ, and he becomes alive within you once more. Her dream, created by her own being who is Christ in her, was telling her she is neglecting herself. Knowing what to do is not enough. Knowledge must be acted upon. It is so easy to accept the Christian faith and use it only as a substitute for action, and so difficult to live by it; but only as you live by your imagination can you ever know who you really are.

I had a similar experience as this lady's, but mine was in another form of the symbol of Christ, which is the pig. One night I found myself in a nursery filled with everything that grows. As I started to leave, I looked down to find a little runt of a pig at my feet. Picking him up, I placed him on a table, broke off some branches of a nearby tree to cushion him, and began to search for food to feed him. Then, as happens in dreams, the scene shifted. I am now in a vegetable market with the pig at my side. He has grown in stature but is very thin. Suddenly I realized that he was mine, so I turned to my little daughter Vicki and said: "Go get me some food that I may feed my pig." She replied: "Daddy, I don't have any money." Then I said: "You don't need money here, for all of this belongs to us." Going over to a stand of crackers, piled in the form of a pyramid, Vicki took a box from the base, causing the entire pyramid to come tumbling down.

Opening the box, I began to feed my pig when my brother Victor came by and, taking what appeared to be white, creamy grease, he spread it on my crackers saying: "This will give it sustenance." Suddenly a lit candle appeared within the mixture and I said: "The candle is lit and it must never go out again." Then these words from scripture came to me: "His candle is lit upon my forehead and by this light I walk through darkness, for the spirit of man is the candle of the Lord."

Prior to this vision I had discovered that my imagination was the only God who ever existed, yet in spite of this discovery I had not fed it. Rather I continued to use the rational approach to life by planning my life on a reasonable basis. Knowing of a power that did not need reason was not enough; I had to exercise this power within me. And then I was determined to exercise my imagination on behalf of myself and others. I saw my candle was lit and knew that from then on, I would not let its light go out or get dim for lack of use.

Paul said: "I am a steward of the mystery." The word "steward" means "the keeper of the pig." We are told to follow the example of the dishonest steward and falsify our records. To be a steward of the mysteries, however, the pig must be fed so that you know what you are talking about. You must exercise your powerful imagination morning, noon, and night and never neglect it.

If tonight you gave a man a million dollars to invest well, he will neglect to feed his pig because to him he has it all. Then one night he will see his pig and realize what he has done to the power within him. If you are a musician and stop practicing for a week you will not be qualified to give a concert. Only when you practice daily are you qualified. And so it is with your imagination. It must be exercised daily and then one day you will discover the Christ within you, who is God the Father, who comes only through his son David calling you Father.

Now let us go into the silence.

Christic In Man

Christ is the reality, the God that is in Man. It is he who breaks down the dividing wall between himself and Man and makes of the two, one new Man. Is this all done on the other side of the veil, or is there something that we can do on this side of that dividing wall? Let me share with you a story of a very dear friend of mine, one who has had most of my experiences. Listen to me carefully, for God speaks to man through the medium of dream and unveils himself through revelation. This is his letter.

"I awoke at 6:00 o'clock in the morning. It was too early to get up, so I decided to lie in bed and do some purposeful imagining. Then this thunderous voice came from within me declaring, '*I Am God! I Am Self-Contained! I Am Self Sufficient!*' It kept repeating these words over and over and over until finally I said to it, 'I know, and I'm trying to do something about it, but you are speaking so loudly I cannot imagine.' But the voice continued '*I Am God! I Am Self-Contained! I Am Self Sufficient!*' over and over again. It seemed to me like rape, if you can't prevent it, relax and enjoy it, so I did, and fell asleep enjoying this declaration.

"Then I found myself in a vast desert of nothingness. Not a blade of grass, not a shrub, not a cactus, nothing but an infinite desert. I am holding some golf balls in my hand. I throw one and instantly a beautiful home and yard appear in technicolor. I throw another and a second home and yard appear, this time with people around it. Taking another ball, I threw it across the way and a wonderful putting green appeared. Then a man at my side said, 'Isn't that terrific. You put the ball right next to the hole.' And I answered, 'No, I don't do it that way. I put the ball down and put the hole next to it!'"

"Then I created a huge gate and we walked through it into a miserable scene of dilapidated house and a streetcar in the last stage of decay. I took a ball and tried to throw it, but no matter how I tried to release it, it would not leave my hand. Then I said to myself, 'Maybe it is beyond my power.' And as I contemplated this scene the ball was released and the house was transformed into an ultra-modern hotel as the streetcar became a streamlined bus which quickly moved away."

It was so easy for me to create out of nothing, but when I came upon a scene out of the past, that I know to be a fact, I couldn't change it, for I couldn't let go of the past. But I persisted and persisted and I was eventually rewarded, as the house was turned into a glorious new hotel and the streetcar into a streamlined bus.

"Then" he said, "I came upon a scene which resembled the Miracle Mile on Wilshire Boulevard with an island up the middle. But, in place of the usual well-dressed men and women, I saw young boys in messy pants and girls in bikinis. So, I decided to throw another ball, and as I did they were transformed into beautifully dressed ladies and gentlemen, dining under umbrellas and served by elegantly dressed waiters. Then I turned to my friend and said, 'You know, maybe I should have left them as they were.' Now, he's a very humorous man, may I tell you, and he always ends his letters to me on a humorous note, so he added, "and I awoke not a moment too soon."

Now, God speaks to man through the medium of dream. Although there were no golf courses two thousand years ago, the word "ball" appears in the 22nd chapter of Isaiah. When you read it you think God rejected a man, but all of these are states of consciousness. God rejected the state, not its occupant, for God is playing all the parts, but we are in states. Then he turns him into the one whose shoulder the peg will be nailed. And on him will rest the burden, the responsibility of the house of Judah and the inhabitants of Jerusalem. In the 10th chapter of I Samuel, the prophet Samuel speaks to Saul saying, "The spirit of the Lord shall come upon you and you shall be turned into another man." God rejects the state of Saul and turns him into an entirely different state.

Now listen carefully to what you can do on this side of the veil to break down that wall between the two, and make of two, one new man. "Jesus came into the world preaching the gospel of God saying, 'The time is fulfilled and the kingdom of God is at hand.' Repent and believe in the gospel." Believe my testimony, for all the promises of God have found their fulfillment in me. Believe my gospel and repent, for the story of Christianity is to conquer by forgiveness, and forgiveness tests man's ability to enter into and partake of the nature of the opposite.

When you see anything in a dilapidated state it is a past state, old and fixed. But you can change it by throwing the ball. If, at first the ball will not leave your hand because of the obvious facts before you, persist.

Neville Goddard

"How long, O Lord, must I forgive the brother who sins against me? Seventy times seven." Do it and do it and do it until you succeed in letting go of the past and seeing what you wish in its place. Persist and persist and persist until you can actually let it go.

Jesus tells the parable of the woman who comes to a constable who, although he didn't fear God or respect man, rose and gave her what she wanted because of her persistence. Her constant comments forced him to give her what she desired. The story is also told of a man who came at midnight wanting something to feed a stranger in his house. The man from above said, "It is late and my children are in bed and I cannot come down and open the door," but, because the man persisted, he was given what he wanted.

You may think there is no way out of your present turmoil, but I don't care how fixed that seeming turmoil is, if you persist and persist and persist, he who is from above has to come down and grant your request. Practice repentance on this side of the veil while the work is going on in a hidden manner on the other side, and the wall will become thinner and thinner until the shell is broken and Christ is born. And who is he? I AM. After you break the shell it's not Jesus and you, there is Jesus only. And on that day the Lord shall be one and his name One.

It was so easy for my friend to create out of nothing. When he threw the ball in the vast desert of emptiness a beautiful home and lawn instantly appeared in technicolor. Another ball and another beautiful home and yard with people all around, then a golf course and a gate through which he and his friend passes. Now he views pictures of the past – a home decayed beyond repair and an ancient streetcar. Desiring to change them he discovered that he couldn't let go of the past. But he persisted and eventually succeeded. He realized that it only took five seconds for him to create out of nothing, but it took so long for him to change the past. Although the ball had left his hand, he felt that it wasn't going to work, but it did, as the house became a beautiful hotel and the streetcar a streamlined bus. Then the transformation was easy along Miracle Mile, for he had succeeded in taking that which was ancient and having transformed it, he changed the boys and girls into ladies and gentlemen without hesitation. That's what you and I are called upon to do.

In the earliest gospel, the book of Mark, we are told that after John (reasoning consciousness) was arrested, Jesus came into Galilee preaching

11

the gospel of God saying, "The time is fulfilled and the kingdom of God is at hand. Repent and believe in the gospel." What he is saying is, "Believe my testimony, for all that I tell you is but the fulfillment of scripture." Standing before you tonight I can say, unschooled, unlettered, unknown, uneducated by human standards, yet scripture, the only reality in the world, has been fulfilled in me. Everything in this world will pass away, but God's Word is forever and his Word is being fulfilled in everyone.

God is not condemning any man, for they are only states, and we must learn to distinguish between the occupant of the state and the state he occupies. God does not reject man, but the state, and puts man into another state. I know that since this man heard my message years ago he has been daily practicing revision. Revision is repentance and revision results in repeal. When you revise a memory that is fixed you have repealed it. He repealed the dilapidated home and streetcar. Here is the new man fulfilling the 22nd chapter of Isaiah. Although the word "golf ball" is not there, the word "ball", that which turns upon itself and repeats a memory image, is. But, holding the ball in his hand (the symbol of God's power and wisdom) he persisted and exercised his power.

You have that power. Test it by bringing a seemingly hopeless case before your mind's eye and revise it. Persist in revising it until you can let go of that ball by feeling the breath of relief because it is done. If tomorrow does not bring the confirmation, or next week, wait, for it is done. And in a way that no one on earth could devise, it will come into your world and you will see the results of what you did.

So I ask everyone to practice revision. Revise the past. I don't care what it is, revise it and the past will conform to your dream of what it ought to have been and appear before you. Then the new man will rise within you and it will no longer be you and Christ, but only Christ. We are told in the 9th chapter of Ezekiel to follow the man who is clothed in linen. He will go through the city and leave a mark on the foreheads of men, women and children. "Follow after him, and everyone who does not bear the mark, whether he be an old man, an old woman, a maiden, a young boy or a child, slaughter them and your eye must have no pity." Then, in the 22nd chapter of Revelation he turns and those who have the mark come before him. They see his face and his name is on their foreheads.

That name is Jesus and Jesus means Jehovah. He only redeems himself. Don't think because of this strange imagery that there are those who are lost. Everyone, at a certain moment in time, is slaughtered because of the state he is in, but the play goes on and he plays other parts and still, more parts, until finally he plays the part of the selected one. And in that final part the mark is on his forehead and the name Jesus is his own. So in the end there is Jesus only. Everyone will be redeemed. Infinite mercy steps beyond and redeems man in the body of Jesus. There is only one body, only one God, only one being, so when you are redeemed you are He.

So tonight, begin to practice the art of repentance, for everything can be redeemed. Now, repentance is not to feel remorseful or regretful. I don't care what you have done; you don't have to feel remorseful about it. You had to do it because of the state you were in at the time. Repentance is practicing the art of moving into the opposite state. You don't feel sorry for yourself and wallow on some weeping wall when you repent. Your sins may be as scarlet, but through repentance they shall be white as snow.

It does not matter what a man has ever done, he is only expressing a state. When in the state of murder he must murder, or in the state of the robber he has to steal. We condemn the occupant as though he did it, but he is in a state, which he entered wittingly or unwittingly. So Blake said, "I do not consider either the just or the wicked to be in a supreme state, but to be every one of them in the state of sleep which the soul may fall into in its deadly dreams of good and evil when it left paradise following the serpent."

Scripture tells us there are two things, which God finds impossible to forgive. The first is our failure to believe that I am He and the second is the eating of the tree of good and evil. Man's unwillingness to believe that I am He is the fundamental sin; for God, whose name is I am, became man that man might become God. My unwillingness to believe that I am he who causes me to breathe, to think and to move, as well as going through life condemning good and evil as I see it is unforgivable to God. But then comes this wonderful revelation, "I know from the Lord Jesus Christ that there is nothing unclean in itself, but any man who sees anything to be unclean, to him it is unclean." And as he lives with it, his state allows it to be seen as unclean. That's life.

On this side of the veil let us practice repentance and transform any unlovely past. Let the mind store a past worthy of recall, for eventually everything that is unlovely is going to be destroyed, and although the mind seemingly vanishes, man does not, for man is God. In the real sense of the word, there is no death for really nothing dies. The actor leaves the stage and seems to be gone, but he isn't dead, for the supreme actor is God and he is playing all the parts. "The deceiver and the deceived are his." I have deceived and I have been deceived; therefore I am both. After I have played every state I am called upon to believe the testimony of one who has experienced scripture, then to constantly practice this wonderful art of repentance.

Repent and repent and repent. As you see someone in need, change him. That's repentance. You could argue with him, tell him it serves him right, that if he hadn't done what he did he wouldn't be paying the price, but do not condemn him. He is in a state and must reap the results of the state into which he has entered. It is only a state and since the occupant is immortal, as you are, you can repent and place him in a different state.

It does not matter what you have done, you are immortal and one day you will hear the same words my friend heard. "*I Am God! I Am Self-Contained! I Am Self Sufficient!*" Right now that same voice is screaming in the depth of your soul. It hasn't stopped since the beginning of time, but the wall is too thick for you to hear it. But when the wall becomes very thin, you will hear it. He heard the words as the wall was breaking, making of the two one new man, thus bringing peace. That's what you are told in the 2nd chapter of Ephesians. "I bring peace by breaking down the wall that separates the two."

Have you ever lived in an apartment where the walls are so thin you can hear your neighbors whisper? Practice repentance and you wall will become so thin you will hear God, the eternal I am in you; proclaim what He is. "I am the everlasting! I am eternal! I am self-sufficient! I am self-contained! I am God!" He heard the voice so loud and so persistent that he decided to test this power, which symbolized itself as the hand where the ball was placed. Then he created, changed and revised all demonstrations of God's power that he now knows himself to be.

Revise, then drop it as he dropped the ball. Release the past and hold onto the vision of what you want in its place. With this power you can completely redeem the past, "And God requires the past." And, although your sins be as scarlet, they shall be white as snow.

Now let us go into the silence.

Q: What does it mean in the book of John when it says, "Salvation is of the Jews?"

A: Christianity is the fulfillment of Judaism. Bishop Pike said, "I am a Jew because I am a Christian. I could be a Jew and not be a Christian, but I cannot be a Christian and not be a Jew." Christianity comes out of Judaism. It was revealed through the prophets and the Judea-Christian Bible, to me, is the only true revelation of God's plan of salvation. All the others are based on secular history. But scripture is not secular, but salvation history describing eternal states through which man passes.

Salvation is of the Jews, as it was revealed in the Old Testament and fulfilled in the New. "Abraham rejoiced that he was to see my day. And the scriptures preached the gospels to Abraham beforehand." Having had a preview of what the fulfillment would be, you entered the state of faith called Abraham, by believing the most incredible story in the world. Then the dream descended and amnesia possessed you. You entered a deep and profound sleep and are now dreaming the dream of life.

Good night.

Christic Is Your Life

This teaching is essentially a revelation of the Risen Christ. I am
not speaking of the life of any man between his physical birth
and death, but of the Christ who has risen in me and who rises
in all. I have no mental image of a being outside of my life, or yours.

Paul tells us: "You have died, and your life is hid with Christ in God.
When Christ who is our life appears, you will appear with him in glory."
(Col. 3:3,4) Here we see Paul equating your life with Christ. You are alive
now, so what does Paul mean when he claims you have died? All of Paul's
letters equate death with a sleep so profound the past is forgotten. It is
from the sleep of death he urges you to roust yourself from saying:
"Awake O sleeper and rise from the dead."

The one and only Christ is your life. Now asleep in humanity, this
power believes itself to be you. And when it awakens and rises in you, it
is you who rise as Christ. God's power and wisdom is sleeping in you as
your own life. God is love! When God died he gave you, his sons, your
inheritance. It was not a home or some fabulous land, but the power of
his love! The power to create every desire of your heart.

Let me start with a point, which has confused some. A gentleman
wrote: "You say others have bodies and lives of their own, but their
reality is rooted in you as your reality is rooted in God. I have a desire
that involves others, yet I have the feeling that they do not want to be a
part of it. Although you say I should not concern myself with influencing
others, as the world - rooted in me - will play the part they must play if
I am faithful to my objectives; but what right have I to influence others?

"Believing that imagining creates reality and that there is no fiction,
I start with a premise that has not one thing in the outer world to support
it; but in the midst of my project I turn aside, for I cannot influence these
men. I now wonder if perhaps this is also their hidden desire and they do
not want me in it. You say when I am lovingly exercising my imagination
on behalf of another, I am mediating God to that other. I know that what
I imagine will benefit all; yet because of my doubt as to their desire to be
involved, should I continue to do it?"

I would say to him, just take the objective. Perhaps because of their talents you have singled them out as partners, but if they moved away would you still have the desire? If so, then they are not essential. If you put yourself in the end by rejoicing in the objective's fulfillment, those who are equally talented - and maybe more so - will come seeking you; for remaining in the end, you will draw the necessary individuals to play the part they must play to aid the birth of what you are doing.

Now, you questioned if all things worked for good. The 8th chapter of Romans tells us that it does. This truth is dramatized for us in the 50th chapter of the Book of Genesis. It is the story of Joseph, one of the twelve Sons of Jacob. Joseph had the capacity to dream vividly. His visions were true and he could interpret them. His brothers, becoming envious, plotted to kill him; but Judah interceded, urging them to sell him instead.

Joseph was sold as a slave, and when no one could interpret Pharaoh's dreams Joseph was brought before him. He interpreted the dreams so accurately, Pharaoh made him equal with himself, and whatever Joseph said was instantly executed. He foretold of the famine that was to come; and when his brothers came seeking food Joseph - now sitting on the throne - recognized them, and said: "Fear not, you meant evil against me, but God meant it for good." So everything works for good when there is time to reflect upon the act.

I could go back to my own small family. There came a moment in our life when it seemed as though the world had come to its end. My father's partners, desiring to take control of the little equity he had in the business, succeeded and our world collapsed. We had nothing and even our friends made themselves scarce.

But what appeared to be an evil thing turned out to be a blessing, for by detaching ourselves from this partnership - which was small in the sense that they couldn't think big - my father started on his own with sons who could imagine. The family has now turned our business into a large enterprise of many kinds of businesses with no outside partnerships, dwarfing anything we thought possible forty years ago when it happened. It has taken time and reflection, but now we can see that - although my father's partners intended evil against him - God meant it for good.

Now, a friend had a dream in which he received a letter with his son's report card inside, indicating that he must show a decided improvement in four subjects, one of which was algebra. Since his son has always been tops in math, he was annoyed and instantly revised the report card. Suddenly angry with himself he said: "I am tired of the responsibility of this power and life's many needs of revision. My son is a big boy now, let him do it for himself," and awoke.

Peter asked the question: "Lord, if my brother sins against me, how often must I forgive him, seven times?" and the Lord answered: "I did not say seven, but seventy times seven." This does not mean four hundred and ninety times. Seventy is the numerical value of the Hebrew letter ayin,[1] whose symbol is an eye. Seven is the numerical value of the Hebrew letter zayin,[2] whose symbol is a sword.

Here we are being told to imagine until the eye is fixed as though nailed with a sword. It may happen the first time or it may take a thousand times to persuade yourself that things are as you desire them to be, and not as they appear to be. But, to the degree that you are self-persuaded that you have done it in your imagination, will the outer world reflect its harmony.

William James, a professor of psychology at Harvard, is one of our great educators. He said: "The greatest revelation in my generation is the discovery that human beings, by a change of inner attitude can produce outer changes in harmony with their inner convictions."

That's in the Bible. In the Book of Genesis we are shown in story form how inner attitudes produce outer states. Knowing the time when the animals would be ready for the act of creation and the watering hole to which they would come, Jacob made a bargain with his father-in-law that - although all of the animals were either black or brown, should any offspring be striped or spotted they would be his.

Believing man becomes what he beholds, and that the same would apply to the animal world, Jacob stripped the poplar trees so that only stripes appeared. Then he brought only the healthy animals to the watering hole, leaving all of the weak ones to breed - the brown with the brown and the black with the black. When the females came to the watering holes and were sired, they saw only stripes and producing what they beheld, their offsprings were striped.

So this lesson was given us in the beginning. Whatever you are beholding in your mind's eye, you will produce in your outer world. It is

---

[1] ע *is the sixteenth letter of the Semitic abjads -*
[2] ז *is the seventh letter of the Semitic abjads -*

just as simple as that. I hope you are beholding your fulfilled desire in your mind's eye; for scripture tells you that: "Whatever you desire, believe you have received it and you will." This is telling you that, to the degree you are self-persuaded, you will become what you have assumed you are.

In the case of my friend, his dream was telling him to continue to revise and not to be afraid of the responsibility of his tremendous power to imagine; for life itself is nothing more than an activity of imagination. When I speak of Christ being your life, I am saying he is your imagination, for life is an activity of imagination. Ask yourself what you are imagining right now and you will discover what Christ has created. For by him all things are created, and without him is not a thing created that is created.

Everything now formed and called a fact was once only an image in the mind of someone who persisted in that image and projected it onto the screen of space. So do not give up the responsibility of revision, and - as to influencing others - may I say you cannot help it. As you walk the street you unwittingly influence people there. You simply cannot stop it.

Another point I want to bring up is this: The prophets who wrote the Old Testament were servants of the Lord. They recorded what they saw or heard, but they did not understand it. Every true prophet's vision is foreshortened. Seeing as present what is future: "The prophets prophesied of the grace that was to be yours. They searched and inquired as to what person or time was indicated by the Spirit of Christ within them when predicting the sufferings of Christ and the subsequent glory. It was revealed to them that they were serving, not themselves but you, in the things that are now being revealed."

Some of you are having wonderful visions and attempting to interpret them in this world. I urge you not to, as you will go astray when you try to determine an individual's departure - for no one knows the hour, day, or season. Only the Father knows and it remains his secret. It does not make any difference how perfect the vision, it was foreshortened. You saw it as taking place now. It may happen today or tomorrow, but you cannot foresee it. You saw the vision. Being a true prophet, record your visions in detail but do not attempt to interpret them.

That brings me to another point which has puzzled my friend. When I speak of God, or Lord, Jesus, or Christ, I am speaking of the human imagination. When asked to name the greatest of all commandments, he did not name one of the ten, but Israel's confession of faith saying: "Hear O Israel, the Lord our God, the Lord is one." The word "Lord" is JOD HE VAV HE (pron. "YOD HEY VAV HEY") meaning "I am". The word "God" is "Elohim" (pron. "e-lo-HEEM") which is a compound unity of one made up of many. In the 44th chapter of Ezekiel the Lord God said: "They shall have no inheritance; I AM their inheritance. Give them no possession; I AM their possession." Study this passage carefully and you will discover that instead of God inheriting us, we inherit God.

Greater love has no man than this: that he lay down his life for his friend. Not pretending, but voluntarily abandoning self for those he loved, God died that we may inherit him. What is He that we inherit?

He has told us "I AM the light of the world." One day you will inherit the experience of being the light of the universe. There will be no stars, no sun, no moon, no circumference - only infinite, pulsing, living light, which you know yourself to be. You will inherit God as infinite love. Whatever God was before he became individualized, you will experience as yourself.

God was a father before he became you and when he possesses you, you are the identical father. The 2nd Psalm reveals the son that was his before he became you. But no one knows who that son is except the Father, and no one knows who the Father is except that son and anyone to whom the son chooses to reveal him.

One day that son will choose to reveal you and you will see - not a David, but the David of Biblical fame. And there will be no uncertainty as to the relationship between you and God's son, David. When he calls you father, you will know that you are God.

When you inherit God, you inherit his infinite past, and from that moment on you will see scripture differently. You will recognize the events in the life of Jesus as signs of the initiative of God in man's redemption. You will understand how God gives himself to man.

John records eight signs of the initiative of God in Man's redemption. Many scholars have put the first and the last together, the second and the seventh, the third and the sixth and the fourth with the fifth, making four major signs. When these signs begin to unfold in you, count the days and you will discover there are 1260 days between the first vision and the last, as you inherit God.

You are not some little thing that God animates, gives life to, and owns. God gave himself to you in the ultimate sense of the word, so you shall have no inheritance, for I AM your inheritance. You shall have no possession in Israel, for I AM your possession. If you possess God, whatever He is, you must be!

I have just quoted the 44th chapter of Ezekiel. Read it carefully. Become aware of possessing God, and you will no longer be the little pygmy you were taught that you are. Don't react to the nonsense you read in the papers. They record the happenings of the surface mind. What happens to a man between the cradle and the grave should not interest you. Whether he is a cook or a millionaire, the best-dressed man (or woman) of the year, or the most highly publicized - that's all relevant to this would and hasn't a thing to do with the Christ in you, who - as your life - will awaken one day and rise.

When Christ awoke in me I was so amazed, as I did not realize I had been asleep. Every morning I had awakened to a new day and retired that night, just as you have done throughout the ages. From the cradle to the grave you have fallen asleep at night and awakened in the morning. In time you have died, only to be restored to life to continue the same long journey. But one day you will awaken in the tomb where awareness was placed in the beginning. To your amazement you won't even remember falling asleep, and never for one second thought your skull was the tomb where they placed Jesus Christ.

But upon waking your inheritance will unfold, as everything said of Jesus Christ will be experienced by you in a first person, singular, present tense experience. You will discover you are the central actor in the divine drama of descent and ascent, for no one can ascend but he who descended.

Only Christ descended, so when you ascend you must be Christ. This is the hope that makes it wisdom to endure the suffering of this long dark night of time. Dwell upon that hope which is the grace that is coming to you at the unveiling of Christ in you, as you! There never was another and there never will be another, for Christ is your life!

Read the 3rd chapter, the 3rd and 4th verses of Colossians carefully. You have died and your life is hid with Christ in God. When Christ who is your life appears, you also shall appear with him in glory, because you are Christ! His appearance is his rising and awakening in you. His birth becomes your birth. The discovery of the fatherhood of God reveals you as the father, and the 44th chapter of Ezekiel is fulfilled. I AM your inheritance! I AM your possession!

Remember: everything you see, although it appears on the outside it is within you. You do not have to be concerned about influencing individuals if you make goals. If you want a great deal of money, see the money within you. Then claim it is yours!

Today a very rich man is getting a great deal of publicity because of his marriage. Born a poor boy in Turkey of Greek parents, he was taken to Argentina when he was sixteen, where he began to import tobacco, starting his business with sixty dollars. He has completely forgotten those days, and the one he would marry - because of ambition for greatness in name - would have you forget his lowly beginnings. Shakespeare had a word for it: "He denies the ladder by which he did ascend." Starting with sixty dollars, this man began to dream and today he is a billionaire. I would not ask him how he stole it. So far he has gotten away with it and it is considered his, but anyone with a billion dollars must have stolen it. It doesn't matter however, as all things work for good in the end.

It should not matter what a man does with his life between the cradle and the grave. The important thing is what is happening within the man. Has the life that animates that body been stirred? Is it beginning to rise in him? It must rise in order to inherit God, for only Christ inherits God. Christ is your life which must rise in you, and when he does you inherit God the Father.

Whether you play the part of a cook or a king, a carpenter or movie idol, is not important - for your external state means nothing. There are men who are now playing the part of a cook, carpenter, shoeshine boy, or barber, knowing they are redeemed, waiting patiently for that moment in time when they can take off the garment of flesh and blood for the last time. But only the Father knows that moment. Let no one speculate as to when it will happen. Record your visions, but do not interpret them. We are all past masters at misinterpretation of the great mission of God to us.

As for me, I have already risen. I am of the world, not in it. My dreams and experiences at night are not related to this world, so I play a double life. While I am here there is work to be done to continue to encourage everyone by telling the true story of redemption.

Take this wonderful story to heart. It is a true one. Christ is your life which is wholly supernatural. The birth is supernatural. The discovery of the Father is supernatural. The tearing of the temple from top to bottom and the ascent into the kingdom are supernatural, as well as the descent of the dove. No physical dove descends upon your shoulder - it is a supernatural experience, but this fantastic truth has been embodied in a tale that man could understand; for, as Tennyson said: "Truth embodied in a tale shall enter in at lowly doors."

Remember what I have said. Forget influence! Take objectives. Conceive a scene which would imply the fulfillment of your desire and dream noble dreams, for nothing is impossible to Christ and Christ is your life!

Now let us go into the silence.

Christ Bears Our Sins

Peter tells us that Christ bears our sins in his body on the cross. And the prophet Isaiah said: "He takes our infirmities and bears our diseases."

Who is this being who bears our sins, our infirmities, and our diseases? Christ! Our wonderful human imagination! When you are in pain, or experiencing deep sorrow, your imagination is doing the suffering. If a friend tells you he is not feeling well, or is in great pain, and you tell him that his imagination - called Christ - is doing the suffering, your friend would not believe you, because he conceives Christ to be someone other than himself. But Christ is the human imagination, and until man discovers this for himself the Bible will make no sense to him whatsoever.

We are told: "In the beginning was the Word, and the Word was with God and the Word was God. The Word became flesh and dwells in us." That word is your I Am! And if the Word is God and dwells in you as your awareness, is not God doing the suffering when you say, I am suffering? Having just revealed God's name, you are confessing that God is in pain; therefore, does He not bear all the sufferings of the world in his body while he is on the cross of mankind?

When I speak of the joy of awakening to the knowledge of who God really is, I would think everyone would be eager to experience that awareness; yet only an nth part will say, Yes! A friend wrote, saying: "My husband applied for and received a temporary position as a carpenter, working for the Los Angeles school system. When he was let out, he said, 'They will call me back for another temporary period.' I suggested that if he wanted to work there on a permanent basis he could, if he would imagine it. Instead he gave me all kinds of reasons why a permanent position was not possible.

"Recently he was called back for another temporary position. When I reminded him of what he had imagined six months ago he did not want to recognize his harvest of the seed he had planted and became very angry. As he spoke, our souls made contact and I heard him say, 'I am asleep and don't you dare awaken me!' "

Her husband, like 99% of the people of the world, does not want to be awakened, feeling that if he awakens to a higher level he will lose the pleasures of the flesh.

A friend, a very successful playwright, with many famous stars as his clients, used to listen to my visions and my interpretations of scripture for a short time, then tell me he had heard enough. He didn't want to go beyond the point of curiosity, to become interested and desire the spiritual world, because he was afraid he would lose his physical contact with life and he was only interested in sex. He had money and everything money could buy, and he loved playing the field in the theatrical world.

He died a few years ago and is now restored to a body just like the one he had here, only young, full of vigor, eager to continue his sexual life. This man has not felt the famine which is sent. It is not a hunger for food or a thirst for water, but for the hearing of the word of God. And until that famine possesses you God's word will not hold your interest. I could go on the radio and TV or write articles for the newspapers regarding my experiences, but - like the lady's husband - they would say, "I am asleep and don't you dare awaken me!"

Now, God and his word are one, so if God sent his word, then he sent himself declaring: "He who sees me, sees him who sent me; for I am the word which will not return unto me void, but must accomplish that which I purpose and prosper in the thing for which I was sent."

The outer man is the external word, which comes first. The inner man is then sent to animate and eventually give life to the outer man by fulfilling the word. And when the outer man hungers for the word of God, everything said in scripture concerning God's plan of self-redemption fulfills itself in him. He doesn't redeem someone else, as there is no one else. We are the gods who came down and God can only redeem himself by fulfilling scripture.

Now another lady shared this vision saying: "I am standing in the midst of an enormous crowd. Everyone around me is screaming, 'He is crazy. He is mad. He is crazy. He is mad,' over and over again. Walking quickly to discover who they are referring to, I see a man standing alone at the head of the crowd. Recognizing him as the man I love, I run to him and cry, 'I love you, I love you.'

"Although the crowd surges upon him and beats him, I continue to express my love. Suddenly he places his hands upon my neck. I feel his thumbs press into my throat and feel as though I am going to die. Then the pressure is released. The man raises his hands, which become two white wings, which caress me with an indescribable love as I awake."

That night this lady fulfilled the 40th, 48th, 51st, 52nd and 53rd (chapters) of Isaiah. I say to her without any doubt in my heart, that she is very near salvation. Everything in her wonderful vision was made visible. She was the man and the crowd. She sent herself through hell because she loves herself, just as you and I do. In Blake's lovely song, "A Little Boy Lost", he said:

"Nought loves another as itself,
Nor venerates another so.
Nor is it possible to thought
A Greater than itself to know."

How can thought know a thought greater than itself? How could you love another more than yourself? It is impossible, for there is no other.

Love is the being playing every part. Love is the crowd, the tempters, and the one abused. Feel distress, and you are abusing Christ by saying, I am distressed. Feel ashamed, limited, inadequate or afraid, and God is experiencing them all; for He is your awareness, believing himself to be ashamed, limited, inadequate, or afraid and dying in your sins.

Just as my friend heard the vision tell her to change the comma, for the statement should read: "Before Abraham, was I am," here again we find that unless you believe your I am is the one you have worshiped on the outside, you die in your sins; for your I am was before Abraham.

It is Christ who bears all of your afflictions, your sorrows and diseases. There is no record of a man who took upon himself a terminal disease while the one he took it from was set free. The implication is there, for - bearing our afflictions and weakness - God has the power to set man free. But Christ is not someone external to yourself. The Universal Christ is a diffusion of an individuality. You say I am, I say I am. We are the same I am, who is Christ, who is God, who is Jehovah - for there is nothing but I am!

Christ, who is your very self, bears all of your afflictions, your weaknesses, and sins; but this is difficult for man to understand. Several years ago I gave a series of nineteen lectures in San Francisco, attended by a lady and her lawyer son. At the end of the series the lady questioned her son, saying: "Do you believe Neville?" And answering with his rational mind he said: "He sounds sincere. He may be sincerely wrong, but I'm sure he is sincere."

At that time the son was living with his mother. Every night before retiring they would remind each other to put the law of identical harvest into practice. When I returned to San Francisco the next year I learned that this man had formed an organization which was in the process of building the largest and most modern co-op in the Bay Area, called the Comstock. This project was followed by building up the peninsula and now this gentleman is worth millions.

Both mother and son used the law to achieve their every goal, yet she admitted she did not understand what I meant when I said Christ suffers for her. Although she could tell me: "I have a toothache," she couldn't grasp the fact that she is her imagination and therefore the cause of the toothache as well as the wonderful co-op.

If you are suffering, Christ is suffering, for his name is I am, and there is no other Christ. God actually became flesh and dwells in you. Once you realize this you will never turn to another. This gentleman has made a fortune, yet he does not understand how it all came about, because the hunger is not upon him. Although it would not be necessary, he is not willing to give up his enormous earthly holdings to have the experiences which would result in regeneration.

You do not kill desire. You do not have yourself castrated. You are simply beyond the organization of sex and your desire for earthly things ceases to be. Ninety-nine per cent of the people here desire worldly pleasures, while I speak of a pleasure that transcends this world - where one lives in a world of reality and creativity. But until that famine comes, you will continue to desire things that die in this world.

Now, another lady shared this experience, saying: "In my vision I knew you had died, yet you had returned to lecture and teach as usual. You were wearing my earthly father's face, yet I knew the bone structure to be yours. Everyone called you the Father, but not knowing my earthly father, they could not see his face, only yours. As I woke I knew that the face I touched on the surface would be that of my earthly father, but its structure would be that of the Father."

There is only one Father. It is He who wears every mask. In this wonderful experience, she saw her earthly father wearing the frame of the Father, because the Father is a protean being and assumes every face.

She saw the foundation, the bone structure of the man who told her salvation's story, wearing the face of her earthly father.

We are told that when God took upon himself the sins of the world, he was a man of sorrow, despised and rejected by men. There is no description of the man in whom God awoke because he is never a sculptured, beautiful man on the outside, but a perfectly normal person.

This lady said that she is very fond of the Book of John, as it seems to be more loving than any other book in the Bible. I will go along with that. She felt that the answer to the experience I just spoke of would come to her from the Book of John. I suggest she read the 10th chapter of John. In it Christ is called a man who has a devil and they question why listen to him. You, my dear, are that central figure, and you are also the crowd screaming at yourself; and you deny the existence of the Christ within, for there is no other. There is only God.

You can put God to the test, and if He proves himself in the testing then you will know God is your own wonderful human imagination. If you want the joy of marriage, a love affair, or a romance, you can test God by assuming the one you desire is with you now. And to the degree you persist in that assumption, it will be yours to experience. Do not be concerned as to how or when it will happen; simply persist in the assumption that it has happened, and when it does you will know who God is.

My wife woke too early to get up this morning, so she thought about what she wanted most, and that was for her husband and daughter to be blissfully happy. Thinking of what she could do to make it so, she realized that it was something they alone must decide. Then she fell asleep dwelling on their happiness and this is her dream: Seeing me lying on a couch she heard me say: "I don't feel comfortable here," and she replied: "I know - you don't like to sleep on the first floor, but would rather be elevated and sleep above."

Then the dream changed and she was putting a puzzle together with our daughter Vicki, who began to laugh as she picked up a piece of the puzzle and watched it fall into its perfect place. Looking at Vicki she said to herself: "I have never seen her look so pretty and be so blissfully happy." Then she awoke. Her desire for happiness was answered in the depth of her being and must now come to the surface.

Jesus Christ is your own wonderful human imagination and his story is all about you. Told in the third person, it is written as though another is doing all the suffering for you; yet you know you are the one who is suffering. I tell you, that unless you believe your awareness of being is God you will continue to miss your mark, thereby remaining in sin.

I am is the key to scripture. Called Jesus Christ in the New Testament, God the Father's name is revealed in the Old Testament as I am. Having come into the world to fulfill the word, you cannot return empty but must accomplish that which you purposed and prosper in the thing for which you sent yourself. After inspiring the prophets to tell your story, you came not only to fulfill their prophecy, but to share your experiences to encourage others.

The Old Testament is a prophetic blueprint which you will fulfill, for you are the Jehovah of the Old Testament and the Jesus Christ of the New. You may either accept this truth or reject it, but what I am telling you is true. Christ is not a little man, but the universally diffused individuality of which we are. So when one awakes and the second one follows, the third will awaken and eventually all of the universally diffused individuals will awaken in that one glorious body called the kingdom of heaven. Having come into and overcoming the world of death, we will be victorious over our challenge.

The men of science tell us that the universe is melting and will one day come to its end. I am not going to question this, but I do know that Imagination came into this world of death to overcome it. I also know that nothing dies, because we are the immortal Imagination who clothed himself in these garments of flesh which die, but we - their life-giving spirit - cannot die.

I cannot force anyone to want my experiences. My family in Barbados all live in comfort and know they earn much more than I do. They judge a man by what he has in this world and are not interested in who he is. They cannot understand why a man of my age continues to do what I am doing, when I could move to Barbados and live in clover with all expenses paid by the business. And I can't persuade them to listen to me because the hunger is not upon them.

Until that hunger for the hearing of the word of God possesses you, you will continue to be possessed by the world. You may become the Pope, but that does not mean you hunger for the word of God. It may mean that you hunger for the power that rests in the office of the Pope, the hunger to be recognized and praised. But when the hunger to experience the word of God possesses you, you will know you - the Word

- sent yourself. You will then understand the words: "He who sees me, sees him who sent me," for you will fulfill God's word.

There must be two witnesses: one external and one internal. The external witness is scripture, and you who have the spiritual experience are the internal witness. Knowing your experiences parallel the scriptures, you know that the Father in the depths of your own being watches to see that all the pieces are in place and the image of his declared purpose is perfect.

Having prophesied what must take place, God will fulfill it; and you - the image of the invisible God - will radiate his glory and become the express image of his person. Then you will be used as the bone structure on which every face will be placed to reveal to the one who has the experience, the meaning of being God the Father.

In my friend's vision everyone referred to me as the Father. Her father was a father, but I am the Father upon which every father's face is placed. She was aware that I had died and had returned, only to tell the story of God's plan of salvation in order to redeem myself, for there is only God in the world.

Now let us go into the silence.

Christic Unveiled

T onight's subject is "Christ Unveiled." That is quite a tall order, for we are told in Mark 13:21: "If anyone says to you, 'Look, here is Christ!' or 'Look, there he is!' do not believe it." And I will endorse that one hundred percent. Listen to it carefully and see the pronoun used in that sentence. "Here he is, believe him not." So, here, who is Christ? What is Christ? Where is Christ? Paul found him and, having found him, he said: "From now on we regard no one from a human point of view even though we once regarded Christ from a human point of view, we regard him thus no longer." (1 Cor. 5:16) He regards him not, from now on, as man. He thought he was man and went out to destroy those who believed in Christ as a man.

Then we are told in I Peter 1:10,11: "The prophets who prophesied of the grace that was to be yours searched and inquired about this salvation; they inquired what person or time was indicated by the Spirit of Christ within them when predicting the sufferings of Christ and the subsequent glory." They thought they were looking for a person, or time, and they wondered whether he would come. There was no reply to that, save "It was revealed to them they were serving not themselves but you" (v. 12) What is Christ? I tell you Christ is "The Way" of salvation. Christ is "The Way" to the Father.

Now we will turn back to the Gospels where we have these events together, for Scripture, as we understand it, says the New Testament is based on the affirmation that a certain series of events happened in which God revealed himself in action for the salvation of man. Did they happen? I tell you from experience, they happened. Not only they happened, but are happening. They are taking place every moment of time in our world. If you have not experienced these events may I tell you: you are going to. Not a thing in this world that you will ever do will stop it. God will not fail - not in one being in this world. Here we are told the events were assembled and Luke, in his first four verses, makes the statement: "Inasmuch as many have undertaken to compile a narrative of the things which have been accomplished among us, just as they were delivered to us by those who from the beginning were eyewitnesses and ministers of the word, it seemed good to me also, having followed all things for some time past, to write an orderly account for you, most excellent Theophilus, that you may know the truth concerning the things of which you have been informed." So, here we have the oral tradition. They all talked about it. These things happened and they are telling it, but come the moment in time that many undertook to put it into written form and he thought it wise to do the same thing. And so he said: "Having observed all things closely for some time past." He thought he, too, would put it in written form for one he called Theophilus - meaning "one who loves God." He is speaking to you. You love God, I love God. He is the source of everything - the source of our life and the end of all things. And, so, he is addressing his remarks to you - O dear Theophilus - that you may know the truth concerning the things of which you have been informed.

And so, we heard it orally. I did as a child, but when I began to read and write I could read it for myself, but did not understand it. Before I could read it, mother taught it to me and I was sent to school and it was taught to me in school. Then I was sent to Sunday school and I heard the story told by the teacher. And, so, we heard it orally. Then came the moment in time we could read it for ourselves. Then came this closed book.

Now, let us see if we can unveil Christ tonight. In Matthew 16:13, one called Christ Jesus turns to his disciples and asked this question: "Who do men say that the Son of man is?" And they replied, "Some say John the Baptist, others say Elijah, and others Jeremiah or one of the prophets." Then he said to them: "But who do you say that I am?" Right away that second question identifies it with the son of man. The first question is: "But who do you say that I am?" So he is asking the question about the Son of Man. Then he is asking about himself. "But who do you say that I am?" He identifies himself with the Son of Man. And Peter replied: "You are the Christ, the Son of the living God." And to this he answered: "Blessed are you, Simon bar Jonah! For flesh and blood has not revealed this to you, but my Father who is in heaven." He confesses that no flesh and blood could have told it, it has to come by revelation. Where do we find this flesh and blood revelation? In Galatians 1:16, 17. "When it pleased God to reveal His son in me, I conferred not with flesh and blood." That, mortal mind could not reveal, no matter how it rationalized or tried to unravel this mystery. It cannot, it has to be revealed - it has to be completely unfolded, in the individual. So, he said: "I am the Son of man."

Now, we go back in the Old Testament to find this cue. Where did God promise this? We turn to 2 Samuel, 7th Chapter. This is a vision. We are told between the 8th and 17th verses, that Nathan received a vision, and "according to all these words and according to all this vision, Nathan spoke to David. This is what he told David: "And the Lord said unto me - the Lord of Hosts O go to my servant David and say to David, 'When your days are fulfilled and you lie down with your fathers, I will raise up your son after you, who shall come forth from your body, and I will be his father, and he shall be my son.' Here, we have to now spiritualize the vision of David. Here is David, a man. If "I will raise up your son after you," then he is David's son. I cannot deny it. "I will raise up your son after you who will come forth from your body." "I will (now the Lord is speaking) be his father and he shall be my son." If he is the son of David then he is the Son of man. If, on the other hand, the Lord adopts him, "He shall be my son," then he is the Son of God. So, in this case, who do men say the Son of man is? And they all thought of all kinds of things. He said then: "Who do you say I am?" "You are Christ, the Son of God." Now right away you think in terms "You are Christ, the Son of God" and yet - the Son of man, you think of a man. And it is not so at all.

Here is a man as you are - male or female - walking the earth. You have heard the story orally, but when you began to read you could read it for yourself, but you did not understand it. You are playing your normal part in this world and one day when you least expect it - in fact, you never expect it - you thought it happened 2,000 years ago to one person and that was it - well, you are that person. It is happening to you. You go through the entire series of events as recorded in Scripture, and then you know (who) Christ is. Christ is "The Way" to the Father - and there is no other Way. "I am the Way." To what? To everything in this world! But especially to the Father. "I am the Way. No one comes unto the Father but by me," as told in the 14th (chapter) of John. But no one comes unto the Father but by me." So, here is the Way. What is the Way? Then you search the Scripture and find the Way, and the Way you do not determine - it was in the beginning. Listen to the statement carefully, in Paul's Letter to the Colossians (1:15-17): "He is the image of the invisible God, the first-born of all creation; for in him all things were created, in heaven and on earth, visible and invisible, whether thrones or dominions or principalities or authorities - all things were created through him for him. He is before all things, and in him all things hold together."

"He is the image of the invisible God - the first born of all creation." Now where is this said in the Old Testament? Because the New is only the fulfillment. The whole is in the Old and the New is fulfillment. You will find it in Proverbs 8:22, 23: "The Lord created me at the beginning of his work, the first of his acts of old. Ages ago I was set up, at the first, before the beginning of the earth . . . when he marked out the foundations of the earth, then I was beside him like a little child." (v. 29) Here is God's way of salvation. But God's way in Scripture is always personified. Every attribute of man's mind, which is God's mind, is always personified. If it is wealth, you see wealth as a man. If it is power, you see power as a man. When you meet Infinite Might - it is a man. All the attributes of mind are always personified, for God is man and man is God. So He personifies this Way - the Way that was in the beginning. This is not improvised. Before God brought the whole vast world into being, he plotted and planned a way of redemption for all of us. This is not an afterthought of God. It came first. "I am the first of his acts of old," before he brought forth the world - the universe, anything - he planned a Way, and the Way was to God, personified as a little child. "And I was daily his delight, rejoicing before him always, rejoicing in his inhabited world and delighting in the sons of man." (Proverbs 8:30, 31)

Now listen carefully: "He who finds me finds life and obtains favor from the Lord; but he who misses me injures himself; all who hate me love death." (Prov. 8:35, 36) Where is it in the New Testament - the second part of what we just quoted? The very first words uttered by Jesus recorded in Scripture you will find in the last few verses in Luke 2. It takes place in the synagogue - the temple - and his parents said to him: "Son, why have you treated us so? Behold, your father and I have been looking for you anxiously." And he replied: "How is it that you sought me? Did you not know that I must be in my Father's house?" And they did not understand the saying which he spoke to them." But the mother kept these things in her heart, and then Jesus grew in years, in wisdom, and in the favor of the Lord. The first recorded utterance of Jesus in Scripture when he was only a lad, a child: "Did you not know that I must be in my Father's house?" He said heaven is the throne of God and heaven is within you. Where would you find him? You are asking me?

Where would you seek me? They sought him elsewhere, but they could not find him until they found him in the father's house - for you are the temple of the living God. It is called synagogue, outwardly. You are the synagogue, but you are the temple of the living God. I will not find the way until I find him myself. And find him without searching for him. One day when it pleases God - for it comes with the fullness of time and he sees in me the ripeness he is looking for - then he unfolds me by this series of events, in his home.

First the birth, then the discovery of his son, and then the splitting of the temple. And I am taken into his home - and his home is within. Just as described in the 13th Chapter of Mark, there is the most frightening earthquake when you are taken into his home, and you are the cause of it. When you move up and move into that heavenly state within you, there is a vibration you have never experienced before. The whole vast world within you begins to shake because you have been redeemed. You are brought in and there is joy beyond the wildest dream you could ever conceive, because one more has been brought into the temple, into the house of God.

It is true as I have told you. So Christ is the Way, the Way of redemption, and the Way is man. "The Lord created me at the beginning of His Way, the first of his acts of old." Before he brought forth the stars or anything, he created a way of return to himself, and that way is called Christ in the Bible. And the people sought him and the prophets inquired as to what person, and to this day, in 1963, they are still looking for a person. You will see it in the papers - they are always looking for some person coming into the world that will be Christ and they are so eager to find a Christ on the outside. They thought they found one in Hitler, or in Stalin, or someone else - always a savior of the world. But, as quoted earlier from Mark 13:21: "And then if anyone says to you, 'Look here is the Christ!' or 'Look, there he is!' do not believe it." You will never find him in another. In no being in this world will you find him. You either find him in yourself as the Way that leads you to God, or you will not find him. But you will find him - everyone will find him. And when they find him, they find him as a "Way." He said: "I am the Way, I am the Truth, I am the Life; I am the Resurrection; I am the Door." There is no other door. You cannot get through it in any other way, and this is the Way of the Father. The Way is enwoven in every child in this world and that child will find the way when God is ready for him, for only God knows that moment in eternity when he will awaken that child.

Now, why are we called in 2 Samuel 7: "Those who sleep with the Fathers?" Here we are three billion in the world today, and "When your days are fulfilled and you lie down with your fathers, I will raise up your son after you, who shall come forth from your body, and I will establish his kingdom." And you think those were the fathers. May I tell you: you are the fathers. You have already fulfilled your day in preparation, and now you are sleeping with the fathers. You are sound asleep, but you don't know it. You came here tonight as a conscious being and you will go home tonight - drive your cars or get off the bus at the right points, you will go to bed fully conscious of the fact that this is when you are going to sleep and that prior to that you were awake. You did all these things conscious.

I have observed my brother Bruce; from the time he was born he was a sleep walker. Bruce would come down stairs and go to the larder, unlock the larder for some milk and bread and jam. He would walk around naturally. We would do everything to make him fall on his neck, but he never did. He walked around the chairs or anything else in the room and then came back upstairs and went back to bed, totally unaware he had done anything unnatural, and the only person in the world who could convince him he did it was my mother. He would oppose us, but not mother. Not that she would have done anything violent, but he could not mistrust my mother. She was to us the ideal. She would not lie to us. So our brother Bruce trusted her, but he would rack his brain to find out why he did it. We put obstacles in his way but he would walk around them.

That taught me a lesson in my mature years when I was awakened to find that I had been asleep all through the ages and I did not know it. All through the ages I have been sleeping - and how long are these ages? Paul tells us in his letter to the Colossians, "The mystery hidden for ages and generations . . . which is Christ in you, the hope of glory." (Col. 1:26, 27) He tells us a mystery - the mystery - the mystery is Christ in us, the hope of glory. I did not understand it any more than the world understands it, and one day it happened. And God, in his infinite mercy, looked upon me and found me ripe, and he woke me. I awoke for the first time in eternity, and I was sealed in a tomb, and the tomb was my skull. And God rolled away the stone and I came out. But until that moment I never thought for one moment I was asleep. Not only asleep, but the sleep was so deep, so profound, I was dead. For when I awoke I was in a tomb, and you do not put anyone in a tomb unless they are dead. So when you enter that tomb you are dead, and you are one with Christ, who died for you. He is the Way. Together you are completely sealed in a tomb. But you don't know it. I did not know it. But I have never been more awake in eternity. When I saw things around about me and saw them all objectively, and they could not see me, I understood the words: "He is the image of the Invisible God." How could you be the image of something invisible? But those are the words: "The image of the invisible God" - the first of all that was created. How could I actually reflect something invisible? It was true, you are the image of the invisible God and nothing that is mortal that looks at you can see you. You are more real than anything in the world. And the whole thing began to come back and I began to see the experiences I have come through and I wondered, for it puzzled me. Looking at you - looking at myself, bathing, shaving, taking care of the body, and it seemed so alive and so independent of any man's perception of it. I could leave the room when I wanted to and do the things I wanted to do but at this moment in time I realized this is not so at all.

When I awoke, I then realized an experience I had many years before. God was bringing me to that point of awakening. In one moment in time he took me into a world just like this and showed me a power that would be myself tomorrow. He allowed me to exercise it just for a moment and I saw people just like you. As I saw them, I arrested within myself a rhythm - an action. As I did it, the people I observed stood still - everything stood still. I wondered how it could be, but they could not move. But when I released the activity within me that I arrested, they all moved on and completed their intention. Then it broke. Then I understood what he meant: "As the Father has life within himself, so he has granted to the son to have life in himself."

So everyone is destined to have life within himself. Then you wonder about these garments and all these things round about us - this thing called Neville. What are all these things? Are these really costumes? Is something being formed in us that is the image of the Invisible God and we have to play these parts and wear these costumes for the moment? I have concluded that it is true - that, as Shakespeare says, the whole vast world is really a stage and all men are merely the players. And one man plays many parts in his time, and the being playing it all is God - individualizing himself and begetting himself, as told in 2 Samuel 7: "I will raise up your son after you, who shall come forth from your body. I will be his father and he shall be my son." Out of this human body something is coming forward that is going to be called the Son of man, because it comes out of man. But it will be the Son of God, and it is the image of the Invisible God - something born in man and he brings him forward. And may I tell you: it is your own sense of I-ness. No loss of identity when you are awakened. None whatsoever. You will know me in eternity and I will know you.

But for all the sameness of identity, we will know each other. But there is going to be a radical discontinuity of form - a radical discontinuity. You have no idea how beautiful you really are. Human face, yes. Human hands, yes. Human feet, yes. The human body - no. Not this body, not for one moment, but I cannot describe it to you. Not that I wouldn't, if I could, but I can't. If I made an attempt, it could only be radiant light, like a rainbow. Yet I would know you and you will know me, for there is a sameness of identity and human enough we can recognize each other. But the form - a radical discontinuity. You can display it and you know who you are, then you return to this - this garment, that you will one day put down forever, and this is essential.

Before this came into being, God mapped out a way, and The Way was called Christ. No one understood who Christ was. They thought it was a man who would come and save the world. (People are always looking for a man that will come and save the world.) That man is you. You are David. He brings forward your son, but that is his son. Then you will understand the great opening statement of Matthew: "The book of the genealogy of Jesus Christ, the son of David, the son of Abraham." Then he brings up the question, "What think ye of the Christ; whose son is he?" The question is not complete until you listen to the past part - "son of David." "Then why did David, in Spirit, call him father?" And you will see the Son of man is also the Son of God. But the Son of God and God are one. "I and my Father are one." You get it? I and my Father are one, and yet I am the Son of man.

This is man, and out of man comes a being that is God's son. And then David - who played this fantastic part, which is now universal humanity - becomes the Son of man. You follow it? The Son of man is one with the Son of God. But that out of which the Son of man comes (who is the Son of God) in turn becomes the Son of man. You follow it? Son of man - Son of God - God. The Son of God and God are one, if the Son of God cannot deny the product of man.

The question is asked in the 16th (chapter) of Matthew: "Who do men say the Son of man is?" Naturally, because He is the Son of man they have to think in terms of man, and they say: "Some say John the Baptist, others say Elijah, and others Jeremiah or one of the prophets." So they mention man. He does not quarrel with that. He changes it, now: "But who do you say that I am?" He is asking: "Who is I?" He tells you: "I am the son of man - but who am I?" They mention "the Christ, the Son of the living God." Then he tells them; "Flesh and blood has not revealed this to you, but my Father who is in Heaven." Then he comes down to the foundation - who is the Son of man? The Son of God? God? It comes out David. That is the promise given to us.

David is collective humanity, and out of David comes the Son of man and that Son of Man is the Son of God. When the Son of God awakes, he has to have a son, and it is David. Jesus never got beyond that age of 12 where he appears in the temple, and they ask: "Where were you? We have been looking all over for you. Why did you do this unto us? And He says: "Why did you seek me? You found me in my Father's house. Why did you seek me elsewhere. You can't find me, but if you find me you find life and receive the favor of the Lord."

When you find life, you will do to everyone in this world what it has been my privilege to do. In these moments I was taken, in the Spirit, and put into sections of humanity and stopped them. Then I released it, and they completed their action. And I stopped them again and they could go no further. A bird. A leaf. And then you ask fantastic questions in the depths of your soul. And you come to the conclusion that this whole vast world - everything in it - is a resultant state of God's first creative act, and this was brought into being as a resultant state, and you are not these garments of flesh at all. Something is being formed in this garment of flesh. What is being formed? It is called the Son of man, but God calls it his Son, and his Son and himself are one. So God is begetting himself in man - his very own Self - and the day will come the individual will be able to say to himself; "He is not only begetting his Son, he begot his son in me, and I and my Father are one." When you are awakened there is no other being but you and you, yourself, awake in yourself to discover you have been sound asleep and really dead for these unnumbered ages.

So when he tells you in his Letter to the Colossians: "The mystery hidden for ages and generations . . . which is Christ in you, the hope of glory," there is a way in man that leads him to glory. But man does not know it. He thinks he is completely awake and independent. I can go back 30 years ago and I would walk on Broadway, and it happened often. I was young and strong. Not a thing was wrong with me, and yet I would walk up Broadway and all of a sudden I knew someone was arresting me and I could not walk. And I would stop in the street and I could not put one foot in front of the other, but I did not understand it, and I would be released and walk on. Then it would happen again - on the sidewalk. I could not move, and I was fully alert and conscious, but I was still. And I know, now, someone was doing to me then what I, years later, was taken in Spirit to do to others. I was being trained and prepared to do the same thing to another that was done to me. I could not move. And yet, I was playing on Broadway. I had my vaudeville shows and played everything east of the Mississippi. I was a professional dancer and nothing was wrong with me and, yet, I could not move. I could feel something holding me - not embracing me - but something binding me. I stood paralyzed. And after a minute or so, whatever it was released me. I was used as the guinea pig by someone using this power within himself as I, years later, used it on others.

So, "As the Father has life in Himself, so he grants the Son also to have life in himself," and he is about to awaken that son and he knows it. We are being ripened - we must all conform to the image of the invisible God. When the image is coming into view, he introduces that being to the power that he will exercise tomorrow, so he takes him in spirit and shows him this fabulous world and he has control over it.

What is the world? It is a stage, but you are not the garment you are wearing. But I will recognize you. There is a sameness of identity and we will know everyone in eternity. But there is a radical discontinuity of form. So, this body of ours - face, hands, feet - yes. But not the body. You are beautiful beyond your wildest dream!

Now let us go into the silence.

Q: The Bible speaks of perfect love casting out all fear.

A: If you came into a world, and you could multiply this to encompass the entire world - but should you come into a place, say, as large as this room, with an audience like this, and suddenly you knew in the depths of your soul that you, by stilling - not them, but stilling an activity in yourself, everyone would be stilled; and you did it and proved the truth of your intuition - who then could disturb you? If you were faced now with the most horrible thing in the world and you by stilling an activity in yourself made it still, and it is so still it could outlast marble; if you didn't release that activity in yourself you wouldn't have to embalm it, it wouldn't decay, it would stand just as it is.

Suppose you were faced with an army of millions, armed to the teeth, but they were earthly minded, and then you stilled the activity in you that gave them motion. And suppose in you, you could change their intention or direction. You could by changing their direction march them into the ocean and when they got beyond sight, you released the activity within you, then what would happen to them? They would be once more flesh and blood and they would drown. Do you know that? But you wouldn't do that, because you would not be afraid of man and they are only men.

So all this is processing that God is extracting his sons from man. It is from man, therefore it is man's son. "I will raise up your son after you who shall come forth from your body, but I will be his father and he shall be my son." So God is begetting his son in man, bringing him out of man; but he can't deny he is a man therefore he is man's son. It is man's offspring but it is God's son now, for this is going to be done differently. This that comes from the world, my son, comes from the womb of my wife; but when my son in this world came from the womb of his mother, he is brought forth from that body. He will also be brought forth from his skull. That is the second birth. There are two births; one is from the womb of woman and one is from the skull of man. That is the second reaching forth from the skull, - that is God's son.

Now the question is asked in the Book of Timothy: "And how will woman be saved?" Because man does not quite understand generic man. The answer is wrongly translated. "Woman will be saved by the bearing of the child." Unfortunately, they put that in the foot-note and they gave as the answer: "Woman will be saved by bearing children." It hasn't a thing to do with any bearing of children. "Woman will be saved by the bearing of the child," just as man is saved. But they can't believe that man could bear a child. He can sire one but he can't bear one. Yet the question is asked in the Book of Jeremiah: "Can man have a child, can he bear a child?" The question is not answered but God answers it by stating that he is seeing, having asked the question. "Can a man bear a child? Why then do I see every man with his hands delivering himself, pulling himself out of himself just like a woman in labor." (Jeremiah 30) And in the 2nd Chapter of Timothy: "How then will woman be saved?" and I tell you the true translation of that phrase is "By the bearing of the child." The foot note uses it and they tell you the literal Greek is "Bearing of the child." But they cannot understand it any more than they could understand Jeremiah, so they say: "Woman will be saved by bearing children." It hasn't a thing to do with bearing children. Salvation does it entirely differently - out of the skull of generic man, male or female. The symbolism is the first step in the great Way called Christ. Christ is the way, and the first (step) is the birth of the individual by being resurrected, symbolized in the birth of a child.

They find the sign they were told they would find when this event takes place in eternity. They will find the sign and the sign is the child, and they will tell you it is your child. They will give it to you and you will hold it, as told in the Book of Luke, and you will have a joy in the Way of salvation.

There is a definite way and there is no other way. People say: "Well, there must be another way." I swear there is no other way. Foundation is the only salvation. Don't try to get away from it. It is the only foundation. It is all in the Hebraic world as a promise. So, it is said: "He opened unto thee the Scriptures and they said within themselves: "'Did not our hearts burn when he opened to us the Scripture,' and beginning with Moses and all through the prophets and the Psalms he interprets to them all concerning himself." The whole thing is about himself — that is, you. Moses rejoiced. He rejoiced for what? "He endured all the fires of Egypt; he gave up all the treasures of Egypt, because he considered the wealth of Christ far greater, and he endured as seeing him who is invisible." He endured. Read the story of Moses. How would you say that Moses, who preceded him by thousands of years, endured as seeing him? That is told in the 11th chapter of the Book of Hebrews: "Moses endured as seeing him who is invisible."

Now we are told that "Abraham rejoiced that he was to see my day. He saw it and was glad." How could Abraham rejoice? Everything was in preparation and then came that moment in time when the first could be brought forward, but from that moment on all are being brought forward. How many in the world? I don't know, but all are being brought forward and not one will fail. So what is doing it? "He who began a good work in you will bring it to completion at the day of Jesus Christ." So the day is coming when that moment in time you are the image of that invisible God, God is bringing forth. He can't bring you forth until you conform to the image of the invisible God, for you must be one with your Father. That you are one with him in the true essence of the word: "I and my Father are one."

9 781603 868082